A
FATHER'S
DAILY
JOURNAL
TO PRAY
FOR
HIS
CHILD

A
FATHER'S
DAILY
JOURNAL
TO PRAY
FOR
HIS
CHILD

DR. SHARON FORDE-ATIKOSSIE

CITIOFBOOKS, INC.
3736 Eubank NE Suite A1
Albuquerque, NM 87111-3579
www.citiofbooks.com
Hotline: 1 (877) 389-2759
Fax: 1 (505) 930-7244

Ordering Information:
Quantity sales. Special discounts are available on quantity purchases by corporations, associations, and others. For details, contact the publisher at the address above.

Printed in the United States of America.

ISBN-13:   Softcover   979-8-90124-158-5
                eBook   979-8-90124-159-2

Library of Congress Control Number: 202690646

You are a human being

With feelings

Emotion

and

a Heart

and

not forgetting

Character.

It is okay to write things down

Lead with character not ego

Treat people with respect

Have a core value

Focus on doing what is right

Don't forget to pray

Many times we find ourselves thinking about various things or having a lot of things going through our minds, or better yet goes to the point where we tell ourselves that we will remember what we are thinking, and will write it down later, however by the time we are ready to put it in writing we forget.

Presented to

BY

Date

Occasion

Write
It
Down

**Lord God, thank You so much
for fathers
and all the sacrifices they
make out of love for their
children. When they feel tired,
overwhelmed, and weak,
please give them the strength
to keep going and the courage
to stand strong. Amen**

DAY____________

DATE____________

TOPIC____________

____

____

____

____

____

*"I can do all things through him who
strengthens me."*

____

____

____

____

Heavenly Father, bless all the dads with Your wisdom, patience, and love. Guide them to be a source of strength and support for their families, especially their children as they lean on You. Amen.

DAY_____________

DATE_____________

TOPIC_____________

____

____

____

____

____

"For the Lord reproves him whom he loves, as a father the son in whom he delights. Proverbs 3:12

____

____

____

____

____

**Lord, we thank you the our
fathers for putting our needs
above their own convenience
and comfort; for teaching
our children, and to show
courage and determination in
the face of adversity;
for challenging us to
move beyond self-limiting
boundaries; for modeling the
qualities that would turn us
into responsible, principled,
caring adults. Amen**

DAY_____________

DATE_____________

TOPIC_____________

_Foolishness is bound up in the heart of a child; The rod of
discipline will remove it far from him - Proverbs 22:15_

**Thank you God for giving
our fathers the grace to
acknowledge and learn from
their mistakes.
Give them the grace to extend
to them the same forgiveness
that you offer us all.
Help us to resist the urge to
stay stuck in past bitterness,
instead, moving forward with
humility and peace of heart.
Amen**

DAY_____________

DATE____________

TOPIC___________

____

____

____

____

____

As a father has compassion on his children, so the LORD
has compassion on those who fear him - Psalm 103:13

____

____

____

____

____

**Lord we ask your blessing
on those men who served
as father figures in the lives
of their children when the
biological fathers weren't able
to do so.
May the love and selflessness
they showed to the children
be returned to them in all their
relationships, and help them
to know that their influence
has changed us for the better.
Amen**

____

____

____

____

____

Whoever fears the LORD has a secure fortress, and for their children it will be a refuge - Proverbs 14:26

____

____

____

____

____

The righteous man walks in his integrity; His children are blessed after him. -Proverbs 20:7

Dear Lord, we pray that our fathers who have passed into the next life have been welcomed into Your loving embrace, and that our family will one be day be reunited in your heavenly kingdom. Amen

DAY_____________

DATE_____________

TOPIC_____________

____

____

____

____

Foolishness is bound up in the heart of a child; The rod of discipline will remove it far from him - Proverbs 22:15

____

____

____

____

Heavenly Father, thank You for the gift of fathers who guide, protect, and love us. Bless them with strength, wisdom, and patience. May their hearts be filled with joy, and may they always feel appreciated for the sacrifices they make. Amen.

DAY__________

DATE__________

TOPIC__________

____

____

____

____

____

Discipline your son while there is hope, And do not desire his death. - Proverbs 19:18

____

____

____

____

____

Heavenly father please grant every father the courage to lead with integrity, the wisdom to make godly decisions, and the compassion to nurture their families. When challenges arise, remind them that You are their source of strength. Amen.

DAY_____________

DATE_____________

TOPIC_____________

____

____

____

____

____

My son, observe the commandment of your father And do not forsake the teaching of your mother - Proverbs 6:20

____

____

____

____

____

Dear God, we remember with love the fathers who have gone before us. Thank You for the memories and the lessons they left behind. Comfort our hearts and help us honor their legacy through the way we live.
Amen.

DAY_____________

DATE_____________

TOPIC_____________

____

____

____

____

____

But as for me and my household, we will serve the Lord.- Joshua 24:15

____

____

____

____

____

Great and loving God please bless new fathers with patience, joy, and the ability to embrace this new chapter with love. Guide them as they learn, grow, and build a foundation of faith for their children. Amen.

DAY________________

DATE________________

TOPIC________________

____

____

____

____

____

Whoever restrains his words has knowledge, and he who has a cool spirit is a man of understanding -Proverbs 17:27

____

____

____

____

____

Dear God, thank You for the mentors, uncles, grandfathers, and friends who step into the role of a father. Bless them for their love, guidance, and selflessness. May they know how deeply they are valued. Amen.

DAY_____________

DATE_____________

TOPIC_____________

____

____

____

____

____

Start children off on the way they should go, and even when they are old they will not turn from it - Proverbs 22:6

____

____

____

____

____

Lord, I am a father, thank you for the journey my son is on as a father himself. Give him wisdom, tenderness, patience, kindness, and strength as he raises his children. May he lean on You for guidance through every season. Amen

DAY_____________

DATE_____________

TOPIC_____________

____

____

____

____

____

He who withholds his rod hates his son, But he who loves him disciplines him diligently.~ Proverbs 13:24

____

____

____

____

Heavenly Father, I lift my son up to you today. Please place your divine protection over him and guide his steps. Bless him with joy in his fatherhood and help him to be a beacon of Your light to his own children. Amen

DAY_____________

DATE_____________

TOPIC_____________

____

____

____

____

____

Fathers, do not provoke your children to anger, but bring them up in the discipline and instruction of the Lord. - Ephesians 6:4

____

____

____

____

Dear God, thank you for the honor of being his parent. I pray that my son feels the love I have for him and that he continues to grow in faith, leading his family with compassion and strength. Amen

DAY______________

DATE______________

TOPIC______________

____

____

____

____

____

Fathers, do not provoke your children, lest they become discouraged - Colossians 3:21

____

____

____

____

____

**Lord our God, please help
my son feel confident,
capable, and supported
today. Guide his decisions
and keep him safe. Amen**

DAY____________

DATE____________

TOPIC____________

Be on your guard; stand firm in the faith; be courageous;
be strong. ~1 Corinthians 16:13

God I am a father, and I am asking you to bless my father with wisdom and courage. Guide him in all he does, help him prioritize what truly matters, and keep his mind focused on what is good and true. Amen

DAY_____________

DATE____________

TOPIC___________

____

____

____

____

____

An overseer, then, must be above reproach, the husband of one wife, temperate, prudent, respectable, hospitable, able to teach, -1 Timothy 3:2

____

____

____

____

____

**Dear God, bless my father
with wisdom and courage.
Guide him in all he does,
help him prioritize what truly
matters, and keep his mind
focused on what is good and
true. Amen."**

DAY______________

DATE______________

TOPIC______________

An overseer, then, must be above reproach, the husband
of one wife, temperate, prudent, respectable, hospitable,
able to teach - 1 Timothy 3:2

DAY__________

DATE__________

TOPIC__________

____

____

____

____

____

It is for discipline that you have to endure. God is treating you as sons. For what son is there whom his father does not discipline? - Hebrews 12:7

____

____

____

____

**Lord our God, please build me a son whose heart will be clean, whose goal will be high; a son who will master himself before he seeks to master other men.
Amen**

DAY__________

DATE__________

TOPIC__________

____

____

____

____

____

Father of the fatherless and protector of widows is God in his holy habitation. - Psalm 68:5:

____

____

____

____

____

**Lord God, I pray that they will abide in righteousness and live worthy of the One who purchased their lives... that there is no other source of life, joy, light, peace... that can endure forever.
Amen**

DAY_____________

DATE____________

TOPIC___________

____

____

____

____

____

Our Father in heaven, hallowed be your name - Matthew 6:9:

____

____

____

____

____

Holy and righteous God please help my children to value work and to work hard at everything they do, 'as working for the Lord. Amen

DAY___________

DATE__________

TOPIC_________

____

____

____

____

There you saw how the Lord your God carried you, as a father carries his son, all the way you went until you reached this place. 1 Deuteronomy 1:31

____

____

____

____

Dear Heavenly Father, we live in a scary world with evil all around. I know that I can't keep my children from being harmed alone. Father God, I need You. I desperately need You. Amen

DAY_____________

DATE_____________

TOPIC_____________

____

____

____

____

____

The Lord is like a father to his children, tender and compassionate to those who fear him - Psalm 103:13

____

____

____

____

____

Dear Heavenly Father, our child is quickly approaching adulthood, and I am scared. I have always been there to guide them and keep them safe, but I know that all too soon, I will have to let them go out into the big, wide world. Amen

DAY________________

DATE________________

TOPIC________________

____

____

____

____

And I will be a father to you, and you shall be sons and daughters to me, says the Lord Almighty. 2 Corinthians 6:18

____

____

____

____

____

I pray, Father, that they have
been listening and watching
our attempted example as
we have tried to provide the
training and instruction to
lead Christ-like lives. Please
guide their heart toward you,
and when they are scared or
in doubt, I pray that they will
come straight to you in prayer
and that they will always know
that they can come to me for
guidance, love, and support as
well. Amen.

DAY_____________

DATE_____________

TOPIC_____________

____

____

____

____

____

But now, O Lord, you are our Father; we are the
clay, and you are our potter; we are all the work
of your hand - Isaiah 64:8

____

____

____

____

____

Father, the most critical request I could ever make is for You to guide our child to Salvation. I pray that he/she will learn and grow in the grace and knowledge that only You can provide so that he/she will come to know and accept Jesus Christ as their Lord and Savior. Amen

DAY____________

DATE____________

TOPIC____________

____

____

____

____

____

As a father has compassion on his children, so the Lord has compassion on those who fear him. Psalm 103:13

____

____

____

____

____

Lord God I want him/her to grow a relationship with You, talk with You, read Your Word, and love You. Please direct their soul toward You and help him/her hear Jesus' knock at the door of their heart. I pray that he/she will enthusiastically open the door to let Him in. Amen.

DAY____________

DATE____________

TOPIC____________

____

____

____

____

____

**Our Father in heaven, hallowed be your -
Matthew 6:9**

____

____

____

____

____

O
Heavenly Father, I come
before You humbly,
acknowledging my sins and
shortcomings. I confess that
I have fallen short of Your
glory... Create in me a clean
heart, O God.
Amen.

____

____

____

____

____

As for me and my household, we will serve the
Lord. - Joshua 24:15:

____

____

____

____

____

Father, only you understand how much I've been hurt by this person... I need your grace and the power of the cross to release my hurt and to forgive those who've hurt me. Amen

DAY__________

DATE__________

TOPIC__________

____

____

____

____

____

A good man leaves an inheritance to his children's children, but the sinner's wealth is laid up for the righteous - Proverbs 13:22

____

____

____

____

____

DAY_____________

DATE_____________

TOPIC_____________

____

____

____

____

____

The righteous who walks in his integrity—
blessed are his children after him - Proverbs
20:7

____

____

____

____

____

65

Heavenly Father, we lift up everyone to you as they seek a deeper connection with You and Your love. Lord, guide them with Your wisdom, strengthen them with Your presence, and protect them with Your unfailing care as they navigate the complexities of life. Amen

DAY_____________

DATE_____________

TOPIC_____________

____

____

____

____

____

As a father has compassion on his children, so the Lord has compassion on those who fear him. Psalm 103:13

____

____

____

____

____

Father, we ask that You provide clear guidance for their steps. Your Word reminds us, "Trust in the Lord with all your heart and lean not on your own understanding; in all your ways submit to him, and he will make your paths straight" (Proverbs 3:5-6). Lead them on the path of righteousness, and help them to trust fully in You. Amen

---

Fathers, do not provoke your children to anger, but bring them up in the discipline and instruction of the Lord - Ephesians 6:4

Lord, we pray for strength as they face the challenges of life. Your Word promises, "I can do all this through him who gives me strength" (Philippians 4:13). Empower them with Your Spirit, giving them courage and resilience to overcome every obstacle. Amen

____

____

____

____

____

Fathers, do not provoke your children, so that they will not become discouraged. Colossians 3:21

____

____

____

____

____

Lord God please my family, protect them, Lord, from harm and negativity, surrounding them with Your divine shield. "The Lord is faithful, and he will strengthen you and protect you from the evil one" (2 Thessalonians 3:3). Let them feel the security of Your watchful care.

DAY_____________

DATE____________

TOPIC____________

____

____

____

____

____

Husbands, love your wives and never treat them harshly. Colossians 3:19

____

____

____

____

____

Lord I pray for all others who
are seeking Your guidance
and love. May they too find
strength, protection, and a
deep connection with You.
"The Lord is near to all who
call on him, to all who call on
him in truth **(Psalm 145:18)**.
Amen

____

____

____

____

____

If any of you lacks wisdom, let him ask God, who
gives generously to all without reproach, and it
will be given him. James 1:5

____

____

____

____

____

Lord, as my family release themselves into Your care, grant them Your grace and understanding. Your Word says, "But he said to me, 'My grace is sufficient for you, for my power is made perfect in weakness.' Therefore, I will boast all the more gladly about my weaknesses, so that Christ's power may rest on me" (2 Corinthians 12:9). Let them experience the fullness of Your grace and power in their life. Amen

DAY_____________

DATE_____________

TOPIC_____________

____

____

____

____

____

Train up a child in the way he should go; even when he is old he will not depart from it." Proverbs 22:6

____

____

____

____

____

Dear Father, pour out Your love upon them as they seek to strengthen their spiritual connection with You. Remind them of Your everlasting love, as written in Your Word: "I have loved you with an everlasting love; I have drawn you with unfailing kindness" (Jeremiah 31:3). Fill their heart with the assurance that they are cherished by You. Amen.

DAY____________

DATE___________

TOPIC__________

____

____

____

____

____

If any of you lacks wisdom, let him ask God, who gives generously to all without reproach, and it will be given him - James 1:5

____

____

____

____

Protect my children Lord, from harm and negativity, surrounding them with Your divine shield. "The Lord is faithful, and he will strengthen you and protect you from the evil one" (2 Thessalonians 3:3). Let them feel the security of Your watchful care. Amen

DAY__________

DATE__________

TOPIC__________

____

____

____

____

As a father shows compassion to his children, so the Lord shows compassion to those who fear him - Psalm 103:13

____

____

____

____

Dear Jesus, I come to You with a heavy heart, seeking Your comfort, strength, and peace. I lift up my children into Your loving hands— please keep them under Your protection, guide their steps, and surround them with Your grace each day. Keep them safe and close to You in all they do. Amen

DAY____________

DATE____________

TOPIC____________

____

____

____

____

____

Fathers, do not provoke your children to anger, but bring them up in the discipline and instruction of the Lord. Ephesians 6:4

____

____

____

____

Lord I pray that you will bless you as you continue to seek Him through Jesus Christ. It is in His precious name that we pray, amen. Please know that you are not alone, and that we are here to support you in prayer. Amen

DAY______________

DATE____________

TOPIC____________

____

____

____

____

____

Train up a child in the way he should go; even when he is old he will not depart from it. Proverbs 22:6

____

____

____

____

____

Lord even though I walk through the darkest valley, I will fear no evil, for You are with me; Your rod and Your staff, they comfort me. Amen

DAY__________

DATE__________

TOPIC__________

Whoever spares the rod hates his son, but he who loves him is diligent to discipline him. Proverbs 13:24

DAY_____________

DATE_____________

TOPIC_____________

____

____

____

____

____

Whoever spares the rod hates his son, but he who loves him is diligent to discipline him. Proverbs 13:24

____

____

____

____

____

DAY____________

DATE____________

TOPIC____________

____

____

____

____

____

In the fear of the Lord one has strong confidence, and his children will have a refuge. Proverbs 14:26

____

____

____

____

____

Lord God have mercy on me, O God, have mercy, for in You my soul takes refuge. I will take refuge in the shadow of Your wings until the danger has passed. Amen

DAY_____________

DATE____________

TOPIC___________

____

____

____

____

____

For God so loved the world, that he gave his only Son, that whoever believes in him should not perish but have eternal life. John 3:16

____

____

____

____

____

Dear God thank you for my family, friends, and the community you have surrounded me with. Thank you for providing for my needs and for guiding me with your wisdom. Even in times of trial, I thank you for the lessons and the growth that come from trusting in you. Amen

DAY_____________

DATE_____________

TOPIC_____________

____

____

____

____

____

But now, O Lord, you are our Father; we are the clay, and you are our potter; we are all the work of your hand. Isaiah 64:8

____

____

____

____

____

NAMES TO PRAY FOR

NOTES

INVENTORY

THANK GOD FOR YOU